Girl, Get Up!

The storm will come, but it will also pass.

A testimonial book for the woman who has experienced abuse and

trauma because hurt people help hurt people!

By Melanie Nicole

Girl, Get Up: The storm will come, but it will also pass. A testimonial book for the woman who has experienced abuse and trauma because hurt people help hurt people!

Copyright © 2023 by Melanie Nicole

All rights reserved.

Library of Congress Control Number: 2024900656

No part of this book may be reproduced or used in any manner without written permission of the copyright owner except for the use of quotations in a book review. For more information, address:

blessed1enterprise@gmail.com

Editor and Interior design by Melanie Nicole

Book Illustration by Gregory Green, Blessed Graphix, Inc.

ISBN 979-8-9878691-0-9 (paperback)

ISBN 979-8-9878691-1-6 (ebook)

Table of Contents

Dedication

This book is dedicated to my mother, my grandmother, my best friend, Donella, and every woman who has been everything to everybody and yet was mistreated, used, or abused. My mother and grandmother, and best friend called on God in the midst of the storm, and so can we because it is never too late. This book is also dedicated to my sweet and humble niece Shattorria. She was such a gentle spirit in a wicked world and served her purpose on earth well.

Acknowledgments

Above anything and anyone else, I have to give God the glory. Without Him, there would be no me. With the help of Jesus and the Holy Spirit, this book has finally been produced. I thank my Heavenly Father for His guidance, support, and moments of failure and success. These are the things that help us grow into our purpose. He has put some good people in my life and some bad. He has allowed me to experience some good things and some bad. As I reflect, I have learned from these experiences and give God the glory for His grace and mercy.

To my family and friends, I thank you all for your support and non-support. Sometimes I would get words of encouragement and a good support system that I could trust to show up and show out. Sometimes I would yearn and look for love and support from my family and friends throughout my life and be disappointed because I did not always get it the same way I gave it. I needed to experience both so I would see that, no matter what, God receives the glory and is the only One who could make a way for me. He knows who to put in your corner. It may be five people there, but sound and look like five thousand in the crowd.

To my church family, New Life in the City, I thank God for leading me to you all. Thank you for pouring into me even when I could not see or receive what was in store for me. Thank you for praying over my kids and me and loving us unconditionally. Your words of encouragement and prayers have led me to finish this book and to get closer to God.

To those of you who have purchased this book, I thank you for your support. I pray that this book ministers to your spirit and is a source to help you through whatever you are going through, good or bad. I pray that you will be able to write or tell your story that will start a journey of healing through your testimonies and experiences in this world. May God be with you and for you along the way. Walk in your Blessings!

Introduction

Life can be hard. In different seasons of our lives, this road called life will make you want to quit. Sometimes there are people who say, "Pray about it." But what if you don't know how to pray or don't have the energy to pray? What if the enemy throws so many distractions your way that you become exhausted and overwhelmed and, finally, you just give up? Day after day, you just lie there or sit there, wasting another blessed day that seems like a year of turmoil and curses passed down from generation to generation. Sometimes you just don't want to hear "Pray about it," especially if the person saying it is not praying with you or giving you the scriptures or resources to help you get on track. Besides those who say, "Just pray about it," there are some who have lived their lives and now, at an older age, they tell you that life isn't that bad and that everything will get better, which may be true, but you are not there yet. Better yet, they say, "Get over it" or "Keep it moving." As easy as it sounds when it's rolling off their tongues, it's harder for you to digest and receive in the season you're in right now. In the time of your life when everything is going wrong, who wants to hear that? You may be at a point in your life where you don't want to or can't hear or perceive what others say.

As you read this book, think of some things that may be holding you back. What are you going to do to overcome these setbacks and distractions? Will you start focusing more on yourself, or continue to hold back your dreams and goals to satisfy the needs or wants of others? Will you allow God to help you get through these trials on your own time and at your own pace, or will you continue to allow others to speak for you?

So, what do you do when you feel like you can't take it anymore or need a change? Girl, you just got to get up!

Chapter 1: Everyone Has a Story

You take blow after blow. You try to get up, but you are attacked from every side and from every angle. The more you try to get up, the more they try to keep you down. From the world's perspective, you are just fighting yourself like a crazy woman or, better yet, a bipolar woman. They will use any negative word they can find to describe the woman they cannot see in pain. They can't see the evil, dark spirits attacking you, holding you down, so that you surrender to an everlasting life of pain, sadness, and turmoil. They cannot see the curses others speak over your life. They don't see the childhood trauma that follows you everywhere you go or shows up unexpectedly at your new address. They can't hear the verbal abuse you endured that keeps playing like a broken record in your mind. What about the physical and mental abuse, sexual abuse, and sometimes spiritual abuse that affects every area of your life? No, they don't know about it, but they judge and assume with no empathy, care, or love. Although there are some who do care, the new trendy statement, "Nobody cares" is what society says now, trickling down to even the young and impressionable minds.

There were moments in my life when I felt like trash—useless and pointless in this world. I became offended when those who were supposed to love or like me said things that caused knots and chemical changes in my stomach, or I pondered on their words or actions so much that I got a migraine. I suffered so much stress that, at an early age, gray hairs started populating in the oddest areas on my big head. It was out of order, but I allowed so much to happen to me that could have been handled differently if I had allowed God in. Sometimes when I prayed to God and He sent people my way to who I could relate, I felt better and was relieved that I wasn't the only one. A lot of times, though, He allowed people into my life who did me wrong just to show me that He was the only one who could save me.

Growing up in poverty wasn't easy, but as I reflect, there were some happy moments and valuable lessons learned. There were times when we had no water and my granny and I would walk the neighborhood with buckets and empty water jugs to a few of the people she trusted. A lot of times I had to take cold showers, which is why I don't like too much of anything cold. There were times when the toilet would back up and overflow in the tub so I would have to stand on the edge of the tub to shower or bathe at the sink. Or the times when I went to bed hungry so now when I get a chance to eat, I eats. I could go on and on about the negatives that God turned into good and actually helped build my character and keep me humble. For a long time, I thought I was alone, and then I realized . . . Everyone has a story. Rich or poor, tall or short, skinny or fat, quiet or loud, no one's excluded. From child abuse, molestation, or rape to neglect in a poor or wealthy family, everyone has a story.

Your story may be annoying to others, especially if you keep telling it over and over with no solutions to change the outcome. We will tell a story to close family or friends over and over again, and they get so frustrated with hearing the replay that they avoid you or disengage. You can see it all over their faces or hear it in their voices. Sometimes they will even talk in third person to politely tell you to get over it or to do something about it.

When we want or need to be heard, we even trust strangers to hear us out. We look for support or attention on social media and tell our business without opening our mouths, or we talk to a stranger at a game or in the grocery store line because they smile and talk back. But does it help? Did any of these people solve your problems? They say advice is the question you already know the answer to. Do you already know the answer or solution to your problem? If so, what is stopping you from getting over the mountain that's standing in your way?

On the other hand, your story can be a testimony to help someone get through their own problems. There are or will be moments in your life when things do not happen by chance. You tell your story, and somehow it becomes a blessing or testimony for someone else. Sometimes our trials are designed to make us stronger so we can help others become stronger. Galatians 6:1–5 (NLT) talks about helping others and not just focusing on yourself.

Dear brothers and sisters, if another believer is overcome by sin, you who are Godly should gently and humbly help that person back onto the right path. And be careful not to fall into the same temptation yourself. Share each other's burdens, and in this way obey the law of Christ. If you think you are too important to help someone, you are only fooling yourselves. You are not that important. Pay careful attention to your own work, for then you will get the satisfaction of a job well done, and you won't need to compare yourself to anyone else. For we are each responsible for our own conduct. (Gal 6:1–5 NLT)

God did not put us here to just think about ourselves and so, sometimes, it's easier to relate to people who have been through the storm than it is to relate to people with no experience. Who wants to listen to someone who hasn't experienced the trials you have gone through? Some people are just talk until it's their turn to see what it feels like. I have come across people in my life who thought they knew it all. They had the "What I would do . . ." or "If I was you, I would . . ." stories, but they had no experience to back up their claims. I often told them, "When you take a walk in my shoes or experience what I have experienced, then we can have a conversation." I used to be one of those people with the answers and a know-it-all spirit, so I knew what it looked like when others did it and God had to break me. He allowed me to walk in my momma's shoes, my granny's shoes, the shoes of the single mother who is frustrated and seems bitter—so many shoes. Why? Because I sat back and judged or assumed stuff I knew nothing about. Even if I knew a little something, God had to show me that it doesn't feel good when the tables turn and the shoes were on my feet. Every time I wanted to or did assume or judge, God laid Matthew 7:1–2 and 7:12 on my heart. Matthew 7:1–2 (NLT) says, *"Do not judge others, and you will not be judged. For you will be treated as you treat others. The standard you use in judging is the standard by which you will be judged."* Matthew 7:12 (The Golden Rule) says, *"Do to others whatever you would like them to do to you."* Does it feel good when the tables turn? No, but it is helping to build our character and control our tongue. I come from a family of negative talk and verbal abuse and have allowed myself to entertain gossip and negative talk, so it is a process that is not an overnight fix, but because of self-reflection and the need to want to get better, I am getting better. There is a time and place for everything. Yes, God wants us to enjoy life and be happy, but He also wants us to help others through our testimonies. Our testimonies minister to others in different ways and are well received by the people we come across. So, don't be afraid to give your testimony and speak your truth, because you never know who is waiting or needing to receive it.

Yes, everyone, from the good girl to the bully, has a story. But who is listening? Who is actually helping or being supportive in the way that you need them to be? Sometimes, no one. Sometimes you must stand alone while God fights for you. It is not easy when the people who smile with you take from you, and when the people who are supposed to love or like you are not or can't be there. It's a blow in the face and a punch in the stomach. But God is there even when you can't feel His presence. 2 Corinthians 4:8-9 (NLT) says, "*We are pressed on every side by troubles, but we are not crushed. We are perplexed, but not driven to despair. We are hunted down, but never abandoned by God. We get* knocked down, but we are not destroyed." Just know that you are important and here for a reason. You are not living in vain, and to somebody, you mean the world, so **girl, get up!**

A prayer to help you along the way:

Father, in the name of Jesus, thank you for listening and sending people my way, good or bad, to help me through this storm I am going through right now. It's not easy to open up to everyone and tell my story because everyone does not want to see me win or see me overcome. Regardless of the storm, Lord I thank you and praise Your Holy Name! Teach me to receive help and to hear Your voice. Teach me to wait patiently for the blessings You have in store for me. Help me to understand that the trials and tribulations I am going through are not to punish me but to prepare me for what You have in store for me as well as for the attacks the enemy will throw my way. I don't know why You chose me to go through these storms in life, but I do know that it will get better, as it did for Moses, David, and so many others in Your Word who came through. Their legacies live on. This storm shall pass, and it will prepare me for whatever comes my way. I thank you, Father, for being patient with me as I learn to trust You more, even when I feel like I can't or am in too much pain to call your name. You know my heart, and You made me in flesh, so You know that I have human desires as well. I know that it's not over because I am still here, and You will make a way out of nothing and turn my painful story into a beautiful one. In Jesus's name, Amen!

Self-Reflection:

So, what is your story? Write down your story as if you were telling it to a very good friend or family member. When you talk to God, tell Him exactly how you feel and what you want to see changed.

_____

_____

_____

_____

_____

_____

_____

_____

_____

_____

_____

_____

_____

_____

_____

_____

List five situations that you feel have been detrimental to your life.

- _____
- _____
- _____
- _____
- _____

Are these situations still hindering your life? If so, what are you going to do to overcome them?

_____

_____

_____

_____

_____

_____

_____

List five situations where you have been a blessing to others.

- _____
- _____
- _____
- _____

- _____

When you look back on these situations, do you feel like you really helped others? Did you feel appreciated?

_____

_____

_____

_____

_____

_____

_____

_____

Write at least two to three goals that YOU are going to work on to help you get through the process. Depending on where you are in the season you're in right now, you may see an instant change or may have to revisit these goals. So don't get discouraged and if you do, it's okay. You may realize that you may have to take this walk alone or find a family member or friend who can be your accountability partner. God will sometimes give us one, so be encouraged.

- _____

- _____

Scriptures to meditate on. Write these scriptures on index cards and post them somewhere that is visible for you to see. Try to meditate on one and say it throughout the day until it manifests in your spirit.

- ☐ "Those who are wise will shine as bright as the sky." (Dn 12:3 NLT)

- ☐ "The God whom we serve is able to save us." (Dn 3:17 NLT)

- ☐ "Don't be afraid of the enemy! Remember the Lord who is great and gracious." (Neh 4:14 NLT)

- ☐ "Who knows, if perhaps you were made queen for just such a time as this?" (Est 4:14 NLT)

- ☐ "When He tests me, I will come out as pure as gold." (Job 23:10 NLT)

- ☐ "So correct me Lord, but please be gentle." (Jer 10:24 NLT)

☐ "O Lord, you have examined my heart and know everything about me." (Ps 139:1 NLT)

☐ "I praise you because I am fearfully and wonderfully made; your works are wonderful, I know that full well." (Ps 139:14 NIV)

☐ "May God's grace be with you all." (Ti 3:15 NLT)

☐ "You are altogether beautiful, my darling, beautiful in every way." (Sg 4:7)

☐ "You are the salt of the earth." (Mt 5:13 NLT)

☐ "You are the light of the world. Let your good deeds shine out for all to see, so that everyone will praise your Heavenly Father." (Mt 5:14, 16 NLT)

☐ The Beatitudes: "God blesses those who are poor and realize their need for him, for the Kingdom of Heaven is theirs. God blesses those who mourn, for they will be comforted. God blesses those who are humble, for they will inherit the whole earth. God blesses those who hunger and thirst for justice, for they will be satisfied. God blesses those who are merciful, for they will be shown mercy. God blesses those whose hearts are pure, for they will see God. God blesses those who work for peace, for they will be called the children of God. God blesses those who are persecuted for doing right, for the Kingdom of Heaven is theirs. God blesses you when people mock you and persecute you and lie about you and say all sorts of evil things against you because you are My followers. Be happy about it! Be very glad! For a great reward awaits you in heaven." (Mt 5: 3–12 NLT)

☐ "The words of the Godly encourage many." (Prv 10: 21 NLT)

Self-Affirmations:

Girl, Get Up! Look in that mirror or wherever you are and tell yourself:

- I am a child of God!

- I am the head and not the tail!

- I am above and not beneath!

- God loves me just the way I am!

- My testimony will save lives!

Chapter 2: The Silent Killer

Depression is such an ugly thing. You may feel it but brush it off as if swiping away a bug from your face. It creeps up on you slowly, and then, out of nowhere, it has you hostage. It's a silent killer because you do not hear or feel it creeping up on you. Now, you are entrapped in a net that you cannot get out of. You feel like you are fighting back, but your attacker is winning, beating you down more and more until you surrender or quit. You fight the D-monster with prayers, scriptures, or feel-good methods, but you can't stay consistent because he is still kicking yo tail. How are you going to get out of this trap? Better yet, do you have the strength to fight back and get out? Sometimes it feels like you don't. Who knows how badly you are hurting? Sometimes no one because you cover it up with smiles, laughter, or social media chronicles. I listened and watched my mom be judged ever since I could understand what they were saying. Back in her days, there was no talking about your problems to no one, so she handled her issues the way that brought her some comfort or relief. My granny went through even harder times, and her grandchildren brought her joy, we were her second chance. Although they are definitely in a better place, I wish they had talked and let out all of those emotions. I know they died from health issues, but also from a broken heart and some depression. God had enough of them being mistreated on earth and called them home to a better place where no judgement, hurt, or pain thrives. You see, we are so quick to judge and hold grudges not knowing how someone is really doing or even caring how they are feeling deep down inside. We lose our touch with reality and when the tables turn, our eyes are popped wide, waiting for someone to understand and bring us some comfort or care.

Day after day, you lie in bed with no energy to get up. You tell yourself to get up, but you still lie there, wasting time. You wake up to the same routine and just feel like "ughhh." You go to the same job every day that you may hate or where you have to be around people you do not want to be around at the moment. You shut down. You do not want to talk to anyone or do anything. Sometimes, to keep people out of your business, you will participate in what they want. Your body is there, but your mind is so far away. Sometimes they see the pain, but they do not know how to acknowledge it, or they are in denial that you are actually suffering. Sometimes, people you depend on or count on to be there may expect you to get over it the way they would. "How long does it take her to heal or get over it?" is what I used to hear.

Yes, everyone has a story, and though some stories may look similar, they all feel different. Your insides are screaming for help, but no one can hear you. You try to show that you need help through your facial expressions and body language, but no one sees you. So, what do you do? You smoke it, drink it, party it, shop it, sex it, or travel it away. You might become a bully or be bullied. You might become a victim or be an abuser. You might start experimenting with heavy drugs or alcohol, starting with over-the-counter drugs or prescription medication just to take your mind off the matter at hand. At worst, you might even contemplate suicide. I have heard people say, after loved ones committed suicide, that there were no signs. The lies they tell. You throw things out to see who will catch the bait because you do not want to let everyone know how you feel, or you may be too embarrassed or emotional to release how you feel. Sometimes, people catch the bait and throw it back at you because they don't want to be bothered or do not have the spiritual capacity or energy to deal with what you have going on because they may as well be dealing with some things or have decided they do not deal with others' issues. "She's grown and knows better" is what I have heard people say, and this statement makes me cringe a lot. Age does not define your pain tolerance. Knowing better has nothing to do with depression and the side effects that come along with it.

Some people will judge you before you can finish telling them your story, and once again, you shut down. Some people think they have all the right answers for you by telling you, "Oh, you need to stop isolating yourself and talk to someone," "Oh, you need to do this," "You need to do that," "You need to get over it and keep it moving," "You need to stop focusing on this and do this," "You need to . . .," and "You don't need to . . ." Are they even listening to you? Can they even hear you? Everyone's talking, and now you done hit the Charlie Brown on them: "Whomp, whomp, whomp." You want to scream "Just shut up" and let out a big scream from deep down inside to release all of those emotions that were trapped inside, and then maybe they will hear you. Now, you are going back into your shell and won't let anyone in because you cannot take the chance of feeling like a loser or unworthy again, like you have no voice in the world because no one understands what you are saying or how you feel. So now you are in a lose-lose situation. The people who say, "Call me if you need anything," "I'm here for you," or "I'm praying for you, girl" are most times, just displaying gestural manners as someone who would say God bless you, please, or thank you. Just because someone says "God bless you" after you sneeze does not necessarily mean that they really want God to bless you; rather, they are showing manners because that's what they were taught to say.

I do not care how saved and filled with the Holy Spirit you are; depression will show up unannounced with no empathy. Depression does not discriminate. The D-monster was sent by his boss, the devil to steal, kill, and destroy you no matter the time or day. It comes through whispers, replaying of past traumas and events, negative thoughts...don't matter how it comes but it will come. I have experienced depression many times. Even as I was writing this book, depression was ticking on my left side, and the enemy was doing his best to break me down, while on my right, I had had enough and chose to listen to the Holy Spirit remind me that I am fearfully and wonderfully made and worthy. It is tough and overwhelming to fight all day long, especially when the issues of life are too real to ignore.

Postpartum depression is real too, and after every delivery, I wanted to just be done with life. My first delivery took place during my junior year of college before I met my ex-husband. I was low on funds, but I had my best friend, a few good friends and my son's paternal aunt helping me out as much as they could. I think I was too young to know what depression was because I honestly did not pay attention to depression until two years later when I met my ex-husband. When my first son turned three, I started dating my ex-husband, and a year later we were married, having five kids within the twelve years we were together. He was physically abusive, but the constant verbal abuse alongside his temper and stance just made me want to run away or kill myself, which was very unlikely because I am too scared to kill myself. My ex-husband (though he had some good qualities about him) was, overall, from my perspective and experience with him, a narcissistic, mean man, and on top of that, the voices in my head just wouldn't let me be. The ex-husband was bullying me, and the voices in my head jumped on the bandwagon to torture me even further. Depression after bringing a beautiful gift into the world is sad because it is hard to celebrate and express joy when you are dying softly inside, especially when you do not have a positive support system. I never wanted to leave the hospital after giving birth, and when the nurses asked about abuse, I was too scared to talk because I felt like it was pointless. I just learned to smile as I always had to do so people could keep it moving because when I cried or had a sad face, they would just look at me in awe like I wasn't supposed to hurt or ever be sad. They would often say, "Girl, you will be alright," so I saw no point in expressing any sadness or hurt until I was driving or in the shower.

Regular depression can be just as bad. From a bad break-up, a loved one gone too soon, a miscarriage or abortion, being raped or molested, family fallouts, or that financial burden, depression can kill you silently because you worry and think about the situations over and over again, and now you have triggered the pre-cancerous cells in your body or have developed an ulcer, high blood pressure, or another serious illness. You are so stressed out that your hair starts falling out, and you either gain or lose weight. You can't calm down your anxiety or panic attacks. Insomnia has taken over, and you are just a mess in your own mess. You try so hard to do anything to bring you out of the entrapment, but you stay stuck. Sometimes, these situations will follow you into adulthood, even when you think you've escaped them and moved on. That's when you rely on other things to take your pain away, which sometimes will end your story. And that's when the "people" say, "But she didn't show any signs of depression or suicide." You told them, and sometimes you even showed them, but they didn't want to know or didn't know how to deal with you, so it was easier for them to walk away. I had a few good friends and family members who didn't judge me out loud, so I felt safe with just them. Sometimes a few is best!

The story of Job is the truth. How many times have you experienced a Job season when every time you tried to stand up, you got knocked down from every angle? Some people are just annoyed with you, judging you harshly based on their assumptions and perspectives, or hitting those "Holy Ghost, Hallelu" prayers on you while gossiping about you or not actually praying for you, which defeats the purpose. Some people won't even allow you to be human. Yes, God made us in His image, but even He knows that we are mortal beings. Everyone is in your ear telling you what you should or should not be doing, but that's not what you need right now. When Job lost everything, from his children to all of his livestock and real estate, he kept his faith in God and wept. Job was human, so of course he was sad, angry, and in disbelief. In his turmoil, his three friends supported him in the way he needed it in that season. Job 2: 11–13 (NLT) states that *"When three of Job's friends heard of the tragedy he had suffered, they got together and traveled from their homes to comfort and console him . . . When they saw Job from a distance, they scarcely recognized him. Wailing loudly, they tore their robes and threw dust into the air over their heads to show their grief. Then they sat on the ground with him for seven days and nights. No one said a word to Job, for they saw that this suffering was too great for words."*

Proverbs 11:30 (NLT) says "*The seeds of good deeds become a tree of life; a wise person wins friends.*" Job had some good friends at that time who just listened and wept with him. Several years ago when my best friend sat me down and told me she had cancer, I felt like the entire world went in freeze mode. I know she was tough and needed a listening ear at the time so I did not show any sign of emotion, and so with tears in my eyes, I told her I would support her and be there for her. Through the years when I would go sit in the hospital with her, I felt helpless watching her moan in pain and listening to the doctors say there was nothing else they could do for her, but I was there praying out loud and in silence and calling on my church family to pray with and for her. Although we did not agree on everything, I wanted to just be there and support her because she already felt alone and unworthy and she was one of the most worthy females God has placed in my life. It's hard living life now without her, but I am glad that she knew that I loved her and was there for her. Sometimes, we just need people to be there because there are times when there are no words that will bring us comfort or healing. Just be there. That's it!

Sometimes God puts people in our lives to show us that He is all that we need. We have to turn to God. Although I was there for my best friend, I knew God was who she needed. Sometimes we get so caught up in our emotions and pain that we leave God, our Father who chose to create us out of everything. His Word is here for us to make connections with and meditate on to get closer to Him. We get so caught up in our feelings and emotions that we forget that God is right there, waiting patiently for us. I was stuck in the middle. My way was on the left, and God was on the right. Most times I went to the left because my flesh enjoyed the complacency, sadness, the filthy words that came out of my mouth, and the negative thoughts in my mind. The enemy presents all negatives to look and feel like the right way, making us think it feels good or is the best way for us, and in the end, it can be deadly or toxic. It was like an oxymoron: my way was the wrong way, but it felt so good and right; it was bad and good, which is far from the truth.

When everyone turns their backs on you, God is right there waiting. Depression will sometimes come and go like a cold does every season. How you handle depression will let you know how long it will stick around. Some people can get help from their family, friends, or church at times, but you have to know or learn which ones to trust. Even with those support systems, others will have to seek counseling, and that's okay. After leaving my ex-husband, my kids and I sought counseling through a center for abused women and kids, and I also sought counseling from three of my former churches. Even now, I have a mentor at church, and not only does Elder C counsel me, but she leads a care group via our church that we meet with on Zoom with other members to share our life experiences and to reflect and expand on the Word of God. Elder C teaches us how to use the scriptures and the Holy Spirit to help us. I had to realize that I could not do it alone because I was sinking. Confiding in someone you trust who is going to tell you the truth in love makes a big difference, and sometimes, talking to a neutral person who knows nothing about you is one of the best ways to deal with depression and other issues in your life. Just because you are a Christian does not mean you will not experience any pain in your life. Even Jesus, a pure spirit who came down to earth experienced pain. Talk to God like you are talking to one of your good friends because He is listening. He will put sources in place. Everyone's story is different, and so depression will look and feel different, but don't get discouraged because you will come out of it. So **girl, get up!**

A prayer to help you along the way:

Father, in the name of Jesus, thank you for never leaving me nor forsaking me. Even though I cannot feel Your presence right now, I know that You are here because You said You would never leave me nor forsake me, and Your word does not come back void. Your word is the truth because You are the truth. I don't feel like doing anything. I just want to disappear, but I know You have a greater purpose for me because I am still alive. Even when I thought about or tried to take myself out of this misery, You blocked it, Father. Thank you for being patient with me. I am going through it right now. I just need some grace to get me through step-by-step. Holy Spirit, intercede on my behalf because I just don't know what to say or do. I need Your help, Father. Please help Your daughter. This depression is real, and I need you more than ever, Lord. Thank you for fighting my battles. In Jesus' name, Amen.

Self-Reflection:

So, what is your testimony? How or when has depression crept into your life? Write down your story as if you were telling it to a very good friend or family member. When you talk to God, tell Him exactly how you feel and what you want to see changed.

_____

_____

_____

_____

_____

_____

_____

_____

_____

_____

_____

_____

_____

_____

_____

List five situations when depression crept into your life. (You don't have to write these at the same time. Reflect and write what comes to you and revisit as often as you need to.)

- _____

- _____

- _____

- _____

- _____

Are these situations still hindering your life? If so, what are you going to do to overcome them?

_____

_____

_____

_____

_____

On your own time, write at least two to three goals that YOU are going to work on to help you through the process, be it alone or with others.

- _____

- _____

- _____

Self-Affirmations:

Girl, Get Up! Look in that mirror or wherever you are and tell yourself:

- I will overcome depression.

- Depression will not take over my life forever.

- I am more than a conqueror!

- Jesus died so I can live!

- I am treasured!

Scriptures to meditate on. Write these scriptures on index cards and post them somewhere that is visible for you to see. Try to meditate on one and say it throughout the day until it manifests in your spirit.

- "Return to Me and I will return to you, says the Lord of Heaven's Armies." (Zec 1:3 NLT)

- "May the Lord bless you and protect you. May the Lord smile on you and be gracious to you." (Nm 6:24–25 NLT)

- "I trust in you for salvation, O Lord!" (Gn 49:18 NLT)

☐ "Submit to God and you will have peace; then things will go well for you." (Job 22:21 NLT)

☐ "God will receive him(her) with joy and restore him(her) to good standing." (Job 33:26 NLT)

☐ "The Lord himself goes before you and will be with you; He will never leave you nor forsake you. Do not be afraid; do not be discouraged." (Dt 31:8 NLT)

☐ "I can do all things through Christ who strengthens me." (Phil 4:13 NLT)

☐ "Trust in the Lord with all your heart; do not depend on your own understanding. Seek His will in all you do, and He will show you which path to take." (Prv 3:5–6 NLT)

☐ "I am fearfully and wonderfully made." (Ps 139:14 NIV)

Chapter 3: Healing

When you have gone through the storm, you just want to embrace freedom and peace. Blow after blow, you just don't know what to do, and you stand stuck as if you are caught in quicksand. Different things in life happen, sometimes like déjà vu. You ponder on the why. "Why me, Lord, why me?" You try to move on with your life, but you find yourself depressed, angry, anxious, falling out with everyone around you or blaming others for what is happening to you. You say it is clearly not your fault, and sometimes that is accurate. You feel cursed and that nothing good will ever come your way or happen for you. You feel doomed, worthless, and just done with it all. When are things going to get better for you? How are you going to recover?.... By allowing yourself the time to heal. Ecclesiastes 3:1–8 (NLT) says,

For everything there is a season, a time for every activity under heaven. A time to be born and a time to die. A time to plant and a time to harvest. A time to kill and a time to heal. A time to tear down and a time to build up. A time to cry and a time to laugh. A time to grieve and a time to dance. A time to scatter stones and a time to gather stones. A time to embrace and a time to turn away. A time to search and a time to quit searching. A time to keep and a time to throw away. A time to tear and a time to mend. A time to be quiet and a time to speak. A time to love and a time to hate. A time for war and a time for peace.

As humans, we are all going to go up and down on a roller coaster, and sometimes we will continue to circle around the block until we look to God and allow ourselves time to heal.

I remember when I finally had enough of my marriage. The abuse was verbal, physical, emotional, mental, and spiritual. I couldn't take it anymore because I felt the nervous breakdown coming on, and I just couldn't take it anymore. The last time I left, I knew that would be the last time, and it was. I stayed in that thang for twelve long, miserable years. Why? For the most part, it was due to the fear of threats that he would make. I didn't know what to do with that. I didn't know how to process abuse. I witnessed abuse in my family, and I would hear my grandmother shut it down, never knowing she was abused until after she went on to glory. This was a generational curse that once I identified what it was, I had to stop it. It took a while, but I had to break it. I also stayed because some members of one of my former churches would be in my ears, telling me I needed to stay or, better yet, get over the hurt he had caused me. One church member told me, "You are not the only one to get cheated on. Get over it." I was just in awe. I was young, confused, and in denial because I always said I would never allow abuse to happen to me. Back then, I had watched so much growing up that I thought I knew it all and was smart enough to see the enemy's tricks. Hmph! I was too ashamed to let my family know what was going on or to try and reach out for help. Then the church family I relied on back then to pull me through just told me to stay and get over it, which led to my emotions being all over the place and depression seeping in even further. I was walking on eggshells in my own house, holding everything in, waiting for someone to come rescue me. No one wanted to get involved, and not too many helped out more than once. Understandable. I had no room to heal from the abuse, no room to grieve when my momma was sick and then passed, and then a year after her passing, my grandmother passed. My mom clearly battled depression and childhood trauma because back in her time, there were no outlets or resources to help her get through what she experienced growing up. My mom got saved just before she passed. My mom and I were finally developing a relationship that did not include comments or distractions from family members because I was grown and understood some things in life better. My ex could not understand me forgiving my mom and my sadness at her passing because she really was not present in my life. I get it now, though. My mom was battling depression and demonic spirits that attacked her, so she didn't know how to be there because she was repeating a generational curse of what she experienced growing up. God had to allow me to walk in my mom's shoes to understand her situation better. My ex, like some of my family members, wanted me to stay in the hurt, in the past, in the negative, but I couldn't anymore because I wanted peace for my mom and me. One of his friends had to tell him that regardless of what kind of mom she was, she was still my mom. I was pregnant with our fourth child, going to court with him because of his selfishness and worldly desires, and dealing with my mom's death at the same time, and he did not want me to be sad or hurt. Maybe he did not know how to deal with me being sad or hurt, or maybe he just did not care. We were both young and our marriage was not based on love and so a lot of stuff we brought to the table did not match up. I am pretty sure from his perspective, he would say I hurt him or did not allow him to lead and he would be accurate on some events. He was an authoritative man and I was passive and from the jump I knew we didn't match but I took a chance. We went through some things and in the end, I fought back. I had to go to work with a brave face because everyone knew what he had done, and I heard the whispers, but I had to stand tall for my kids and myself because nobody else was going to stand for us. I was told by my ex and many others to get over it because it's life and that I had to keep it moving. Those words did not bring healing. I felt like I was bleeding out and people were just dodging the hurt they saw in me. I had a few good friends who tried their best to cheer me up, but at that point, I chose to stop pretending because the hurt was eating me up inside like a leech as I carried another innocent baby in my womb. Not only was I depressed, but I was also angry at God, and I made sure to let Him know that. I stopped reading my Bible and praying, but I did not stop talking to God. I let Him know how I felt every day, and He told me it was okay to be angry at Him but not to stay there. He was patient with me. I talked to Him every day, and months after having my baby, I started to feel a little better day by day. It took some time, and I'm still not over the death of my mom because she was only fifty-two, so young, and her death was unexpected, but I'm learning.

Everyone's healing process is different. Some people can get over it and keep it moving right away. But trust me when I say the bandages will come off soon and you will be backed into a corner if you keep covering up the pain, the worries, the heartaches, the disappointments.... Healing takes time, like a cut on your arm, a foot in a cast, a knee recovering from surgery, or a woman who just delivered a baby. When people are selfish, they only want to get their needs and wants satisfied, not caring how you feel or what you need or want. When you keep putting a bandage over a cut or sore and don't allow time for it to get some air and breathe, the sore will take longer to heal.

So, after I left my ex, I called myself jumping out into the dating world-a world I wasn't ready for because I was used to being in a long-term relationship. One of my friends told me I had an institutionalized mindset because although I was divorced and free, I acted as if the doors were still locked even though I saw them open. I got some advice from some of my single friends and did things my way although I know I was not ready to date because I didn't allow myself time to heal, so everyone I tried to date ended up getting kicked to the curb. Some of the men were really good guys, but as soon as my mind started wandering, I would see myself getting abused or cheated on all over again, and I just couldn't allow that to happen. I also met some guys who I knew were no good. They played on my emotions, and my mental stability and insecurities went through the roof. I was already battling insecurities from my childhood, and I allowed these selfish takers to do just that—take. I asked one guy how he could repeatedly call me beautiful, tell me I was a good woman and mom, and that he appreciated me, but then treat me like the dirt he walked on, and he said, "Oh, I am so sorry. I don't mean to make you feel bad, but I'm just living in the moment!" The only things I got from that situation were a broken heart and a lesson learned. After dealing with that one guy, the depression I was already dealing with from my ugly divorce, my financial struggles while trying to hold it down with six kids who were dealing with their own emotions, and my preexisting insecurities and feelings of unworthiness and feeling cursed just got worse. Anything that triggered my memory of my childhood trauma and a few relationship stings would make me call it quits, run away, and isolate myself. One of my friends had a workshop titled #PainNoMore through her M.E.N.D organization and I met a presenter there that did a presentation that helped me begin my journey of healing. I look back and all I can say is thank you, Lord, for saving me because I was a fool to entertain such nonsense and believe that everyone was worthy of my time and energy. God gave me a new church family who really teach the Word without judgement and with lots of love because He saw where I was headed if I continued to stay stuck in my feelings and do things my way.

Since I was a little girl, I sacrificed my happiness and time for others, and now I can't get that time back. So now I have to do what I can with what I have and push forward. When I would zone in on my issues and what I did not have, I would be reminded of Paul and his hardships. In II Corinthians 12:7–10, Paul stated,

"So to keep me from becoming proud, I was given a thorn in my flesh, a messenger from satan to torment me and keep me from becoming proud. Three different times I begged the Lord to take it away. Each time He said, "My grace is all you need. My power works best in weakness". So now I am glad to boast about my weaknesses, so that the power of Christ can work through me. That's why I take pleasure in my weaknesses, and in the insults, hardships, persecutions, and troubles that I suffer for Christ. For when I am weak, then I am strong."

When I focused in on my issues, God let me know that I would be okay, and He waited patiently for me although I was a mess in the mess I allowed or created. I was the prodigal daughter and when I came back to my Father, He accepted me with open arms. I am reminded of Luke 15: 10-24 when I mess up and yet God stays the same and loves me unconditionally. Luke 15: 10-24 states:

"In the same way, there is joy in the presence of God's angels when even one sinner repents. To illustrate the point further, Jesus told them this story: "A man had two sons. The younger son told his father, 'I want my share of your estate now before you die.' So his father agreed to divide his wealth between his sons. "A few days later this younger son packed all his belongings and moved to a distant land, and there he wasted all his money in wild living. About the time his money ran out, a great famine swept over the land, and he began to starve. He persuaded a local farmer to hire him, and the man sent him into his fields to feed the pigs. The young man became so hungry that even the pods he was feeding the pigs looked good to him. But no one gave him anything. When he finally came to his senses, he said to himself, 'At home even the hired servants have enough food to spare, and here I am dying of hunger! I will go home to my father and say, "Father, I have sinned against both heaven and you, and am no longer worthy of being called your son. Please take me on as a hired servant. So he returned home to his father. And while he was still a long way off, his father saw him

coming. Filled with love and compassion, he ran to his son, embraced him, and kissed him, His son said to him, 'Father, I have sinned against both heaven and you, and I am no longer worthy of being called your son.' But his father said to his servants, 'Quick! Bring the finest robe in the house and put it on him. Get a ring for his finger and sandals for his feet. And kill the calf we have been fattening We must celebrate with a feast, for this son of mine was dead and has now returned to life. He was lost, but now he is found.' So the party began.

Regardless of what is going on in our lives, God remains the same. His love is unconditional, and He receives us with open arms. Others may be mad at how God loves us and forgives us or may want us to be punished and suffer for eternity, but God wants us to enjoy His grace and mercy. My healing process and yours will not look or feel the same, so take your time, take deep breaths, meditate on scriptures, do things that make YOU happy, and allow yourself to heal on your own time and not the world's time. For those who do not have the patience, time, or energy to allow you to heal, well, I would tell you to tell them to kick rocks, but that can cause some problems that, in the future, you may not want to have. Some of my family members or friends could not understand what I was going through, and they did not have the patience to deal with me where I was, so I did have to separate myself in order to keep the little mental stability I had left. I have had my Job seasons and Joshua moments. I am no Bible scholar, but I will say that God has either placed scriptures in my spirit or sent others to tell me about certain scriptures to read. One book in the Bible that I find encouraging is the book of Joshua. Joshua was chosen to take over for Moses, and he was scared. Fear will cause us to stay stuck when we are meant to move forward. Whatever you are going through, God wants us to be strong and courageous. God said in Joshua 1: 4, 6–9 NLT,

"No one will be able to stand against you as long as you live . . . I will not fail you or abandon you . . . Be strong and courageous, for you will lead these people to possess all the land I swore to their ancestors I would give them. Be strong and very courageous . . . study this Book of Instruction continually. Meditate on it day and night so you will be sure to obey everything written in it. Only then will you prosper and succeed in all you do. This is my command-be strong and courageous! Do not be afraid or discouraged. For the Lord your God is with you wherever you go."

I was recently cleaning up and throwing away some old papers when I came across a note a former church member gave me. He saw me hurting while in my marriage, but he also wanted to remain respectful and neutral. The note had two scriptures on it, and I want to say it is twelve years old. One was 1Peter 5:7 NLT, which states, *"Give all your worries and cares to God, for He cares about you."* The second scripture was Matthew 11:28–30 NLT, which states, "Then Jesus said, *'Come to me, all of you who are weary and carry heavy burdens, and I will give you rest. Take My yoke upon you. Let Me teach you, because I am humble and gentle at heart, and you will find rest for your souls. For My yoke is easy to bear, and my burden I give you is light."* Back then, the hurt was cutting so deep that I could not comprehend the meaning of the scriptures, but now they make so much sense. I was so caught up in myself that I could not receive anything to allow healing back then. Twelve years later, I just got tired of hurting and just wanted healing so I could have peace. Some of that peace involved me forgiving my ex-husband. As much as I wanted him to suffer for the hurt and pain he caused me over the years, I had to let go and let God. I wanted to hurt him through the flesh by making slick comments and bringing up the past that he had released because I was still hurting, and I felt he didn't acknowledge the pain that was holding me down so I wanted to keep refreshing his memory. You see the point of view this is from- "I", first person. I leaned to my own understanding. I was focused on me and lost a lot of my blessings in the process, circling around the block because "I" was trying to do it my way instead of God's way. Yes, I am human and, in the flesh, but "I" wanted him to be punished, forgetting that I have done some things that would cause me to be punished probably the same way. So, I had to release him back to God and forgive him so that I could experience the peace I was supposed to have because in Proverbs 3: 5-6 it says *"Trust in the Lord with all your heart; do not depend on your own understanding. Seek His will in all you do, and He will show you which path to take."* I wish my ex the best and the blessings God has in store for him because he is also a human in the flesh with emotions and feelings and God did not put me here to condemn anyone, but to pray for them and help them. It took some time, and I am still learning, but I have peace.

Being strong and courageous may mean you have to stand firm and let others know that your life matters too, even if they do not like it. I suggest that you part ways with those people for a while, allowing you the time to get it together, and if they were meant to be in every season of your life, they will be there as if nothing happened. If they love you and want to see you grow and prosper, then they will understand and be there. When we are healed, we learn to let go. Letting go is hard, and sometimes there are some things we will never forget, but when we let go, we free ourselves from the pain and trauma that want to hold us hostage. Letting go may mean apologizing to the people that hurt you and owe you an apology. They may try to use the apology to their advantage and think they have one up on you, but remember, you are not apologizing for them but for you because you need peace and need God's grace and mercy. Let God handle those who seek apologies for selfish reasons or try to take advantage of your emotions by belittling you or making you feel unworthy. You can ask God to forgive them and to heal them from whatever pains and struggles they continue to carry like the shadow on the wall. Whatever it is that you need healing from, identify it, accept it, and release it. There is only one you, so girl, just breathe and heal. God's gonna bring you out of that thang in due time, with patience and love, but you have to take time for you to heal. So, **girl, get up and be healed!**

A prayer to help you along the way:

Father, in the name of Jesus, I come to you with a broken heart and a broken spirit. I need healing from the abuse, neglect, financial struggle, insecurity, low self-esteem, feeling of unworthiness, and everything else that seems to go wrong in my life. Help me seek Your face and do Your will. Place the right people and scriptures from Your Word in my life in this season so that I can heal. Remove those people, barriers, and negative energies out of my life that are hanging on with no purpose. You said Your Word does not come back void, and I believe my healing is taking place. I thank you, in Jesus' name, Amen!

Self-Reflection:

What is it that you need to heal from? Write down your story as if you were telling it to a very good friend or family member. When you talk to God, tell Him exactly how you feel and what you want to see changed. List some situations that caused your open wounds to stay open. (You don't have to write these at the same time. Reflect and write what comes to you and revisit as often as you need to.)

* _____

* _____

* _____

* _____

* _____

Are these situations still hindering your life? If so, what are you going to do to overcome them?

_____

_____

_____

_____

_____

On your own time, write at least two to three goals that YOU are going to work on to help you through the process be it alone or with others.

- _____

- _____

- _____

Scriptures to meditate on:

☐ "I have told you all this so that you may have peace in Me. Here on earth you will have many trials and sorrows. But take heart, because I have overcome the world." (John 16:33 NLT)

☐ "Come to me, all of you who are weary and carry heavy burdens, and I will give you rest. Take My yoke upon you. Let Me teach you, because I am humble and gentle at heart, and you will find rest for your souls. For My yoke is easy to bear, and the burden I give you is light." (Mt 11:28–30 NLT)

☐ "The Lord is good, a Strong Refuge when trouble comes. He is closer to those who trust in Him." (Na 1:7 NLT)

☐ "Return to me, and I will return to you, says the Lord of Heaven's Armies." (Zee 1:3 NLT)

☐ "Even when I walk through the darkest valley, I will not be afraid, for you are close beside me. Your rod and Your staff protect and comfort me." (Ps 23:4 NLT)

☐ "May God our Father and the Lord Jesus Christ give you grace and peace." (I Cor 1:3 NLT)

☐ "I have suffered much O Lord; restore my life again as You have promised. Lord, accept my offering of praise and teach me your regulations. My life constantly hangs in the balance, but I will not stop obeying your instructions. The wicked have set their traps for me, but I will not turn from your commandments." (Ps 119: 106–110 NLT)

☐ "He sent out His word and healed them, snatching them from the door of death." (Ps 107:36 NLT)

☐ "Create in me a clean heart O God, renew a loyal spirit within me." (Ps 51:10 NLT)

☐ "My suffering was good for me for it taught me to pay attention to your decrees." (Ps 119:71 NLT)

☐ "I have heard your prayer and seen your tears. I will heal you." (2 Kings 20:5 NLT)

☐ "He heals the brokenhearted and bandages their wounds." (Ps 147: 3 NLT)

☐ "In my distress I cried out to the Lord; yes, I prayed to my God for help. He heard me from His sanctuary; my cry to Him reached His ears." (Ps 18:6 NLT)

Self-Affirmations:

Girl, Get Up! Look in the mirror or wherever you are and say:

- I am healed.

- I am more than a conqueror!

- I am the head and not the tail!

- I am God's child!

- I am free!

- I am worthy!

- I am treasured!

- I am precious!

- I am unique!

- I am who God made me to be!

Chapter 4: Guard Your Heart

It's easy to get pulled into situations that you know are wrong, and the Spirit confirms it. You might feel a chill run down your arm or spine, or you might feel some butterflies in your stomach. When you try to be everything to everybody, you are setting yourself up for failure. You help everyone jump over the brick wall, but no one is there to push or lift you up. We give of ourselves constantly. We take abuse that we shouldn't and don't even have to tolerate. We come across the "takers." Takers will come and take from you like a bloodsucker or leech. They will take your time, money, or energy without a care in the world because their only purpose is to take. You have let the "takers" come drain you dry, and now you have nothing left for you. You are frustrated, broke, broken, overwhelmed, and taken advantage of. How do you handle situations that make you feel taken advantage of? You guard your heart. Proverbs 4:23 NLT says, "*Guard your heart above all else, for it determines the course of your life.*" We pour out too much love, too much help, too much of our time, energy, or money and then get hurt in the end when we don't receive it back the same way. II Corinthians 9:7 NLT says, "*God loves a person who gives cheerfully.*"

We give of ourselves cheerfully all the time, but we have to allow our spirit to speak to us so we know when to cut it off. Sometimes God tells us to help others, but He didn't say to be a sucker. Listen to your spirit because it will let you know how far to go or whether to even give of yourself or not. We ignore the Spirit at times, knowing full well that we are supposed to say no.

So many times I have allowed my heart to determine the course of my life. This caused me great pain. I would worry too much, stress myself out, develop insomnia, depression, and so on. I would spend money I didn't even have. I would try to sleep it, sex it, and shop it away, but just like a high, once you're sober, the pain is still there, staring you in the face. I would allow others to hurt me and allow myself to get so overworked and overwhelmed that I would take it out on my kids by screaming, yelling, sometimes cussing at them, and then isolating myself from everyone. I would allow my emotions to take over and get all out of character, saying things like "Don't make me step out of my Christian box." I would be the one walking around mad and upset, replaying who was right or wrong, going back and forth with people, just wasting my time. The situations did not bother the other person that much or at all, and I was still puffed up, stressed, and misrepresenting

Jesus in the worst way. I am no saint because I have snapped back plenty of times. I would be so depressed by what I would allow others to do to me that the depression had me looking like a zombie. I started isolating myself from family and friends and did not want to be bothered. If I was rich, I would have just laid in bed all day, but because I didn't have it like that, I would have to force myself to get up and keep repeating to myself "Girl….get up!", or my kids would make sure I got up to give them some attention, take them to school, or feed them. My heart was in agony. I could feel the pinches on my heart as if someone was sticking a thin sewing needle in it, jab by jab. I didn't guard my heart from loved ones, from those who were supposed to care, from financial burdens, disappointments, or the loss of loved ones. I could keep going, but the point is that this heart of mine was opened to setbacks, disappointments, and whatever blow there was to hurt me, irk me, or just bring me down. I was better than this, but because I didn't guard my heart, I allowed myself to be snatched back ten miles when I should have been up a hundred. I would talk to God and read His Word, but I did nothing with it but complain and have pity on myself. I would say to myself, "Why me? This is too much. I can't do this anymore!"

I remember one time I asked my ex-husband why he wasn't giving me money to help out with the kids, and I ran down my list of bills, and he said to me, "Those are your problems, not mine and where are all these godparents or friends you supposed to have?" Then my kids would come to the apartment and say, "You over here struggling while our daddy saving his money and living the good life." I looked for people I was there for in their times of need to help and support me, the same way I was there for them and got hurt in the end because most of the time, I could not find one. I would wait until my kids went to bed and cry my eyes out. I asked God when my breakthrough was coming because I have been suffering since I came out the womb. "Why, Lord, are you allowing this man and others to continue to hurt me because I know you see me struggling to keep a roof over my kids' heads and provide for them? Why does he get to live good while I struggle?" I was angry at God again. I just couldn't understand how the child He said He loved was allowed to struggle. It was not my fault what my ex-husband did, but I felt I was getting punished for leaving the marriage. My ex-husband would often quote a scripture to me and my kids that said "God hates divorce." I was so tired of hearing it because I was wondering why I would be punished for divorcing him when he was the one in the wrong. The scripture said in Malachi 2:13–16 NLT,

"Here is another thing you do. You cover the Lord's altar with tears, weeping, and groaning because He pays no attention to your offerings and doesn't accept them with pleasure. You cry out, "Why doesn't the Lord accept my worship?" I'll tell you why! Because the Lord witnessed the vows you and your wife made when you were young. But you have been unfaithful to her, though she remained your faithful partner, the wife of your marriage vows. Didn't the Lord make you one with your wife? In body and spirit are you His." And what does he want? Godly children from your union. "So guard your heart; remain loyal to the wife of your youth. For I hate divorce!" says the Lord, the God of Israel. "To divorce your wife is to overwhelm her with cruelty," says the Lord of Heaven's Armies. So guard your heart; do not be unfaithful to your wife."

Get to know God for yourself. My ex tried to blame me for the divorce without taking accountability for his actions. I got stuck in my emotions instead of allowing God to handle the situation and it took a toll on me. I got excited when I saw my ex being punished and God had to allow me to experience more pain on top of pain because of my self-righteous attitude. I am no saint, and neither was my ex-husband but I wanted him to be punished for every hurt he had caused me, forgetting that I hurt others and caused pain. Night after night, I would sob in my bed, focusing on the pain I was feeling and what I did not have, forgetting about all the blessings I did have. I was reminded of the story of Elijah in I Kings 19, when he fled for his life and was so frustrated and overwhelmed with fear that he told God to take his life. In the midst of him running for his life, it says in I Kings 19:12 NLT, *"And after the earthquake there was a fire, but the Lord was not in the fire. And after the fire there was the sound of a gentle whisper."* Instantly, in the midst of me sobbing in a quiet, dark room, Jesus' response was, "I don't take sides. If he comes to me with a genuine heart with faith and prayer, I will forgive and respond, and if you come to me the same way, I will forgive and respond." Instantly, I set up like a big girl, and all my tears were dried up as if Jesus wiped them off my face Himself. Although those were the words I did not want to hear, I had to eat them up and swallow them because He was right. I had to learn to guard my heart, because if I didn't, then I would be the one swallowed up in a world of misery that would soon take me out before my time on earth was to expire. Not only should you guard your heart from others, but also from yourself. The flesh thrives off wants and as long as you only think about self, you will never seek God and what He has in store for you. I had to learn to focus less on what others had and were doing, and more on guarding my heart from the distractions that tried to keep me entrapped. God wants you to do the same thing. Yes, distractions and trouble will come your way, but thank God that they will not last always. God has so much in store for you if you just believe and allow Him to do what He needs to do. He's calling you higher and wants you to seek Him more so He can bless you more! **So girl, after all else fails and you get tired of being tired, guard your heart and Get Up!**

Prayer to help you along the way:

Father God in the name of Jesus, I come to you standing in the need of prayer. Father, I ask that you guard my heart from those who purposefully try to hurt and attack me and from myself when I selfishly just think about me. Remove those things or people that are not supposed to be in my seasons of life and help me gain wisdom and understanding from those I have already encountered, including my blood family. Lord, I ask that you superimpose Your will over evil spirits and help me keep my eyes focused on You. Holy Spirit, please intercede on my behalf when I know not what to pray for. I receive that my heart is guarded with wisdom and understanding in Jesus' name, Amen!

Self-Reflection

How many times have we let someone, or something decide our course in life because we did not guard our heart? Your predator comes to devour you because you stand out as weak prey, no matter how strong you think you are. The name "predator" sounds harsh but can come in the most attractive way. What are the things, people, or situations that allowed you to open your heart and let it get trumped over and stumped on because you did not guard it? This is your book and your space to reflect on you and what you want to come out of or break through. Write them down.

_____

_____

_____

_____

_____

_____

_____

_____

_____

_____

_____

_____

_____

_____

_____

_____

_____

List some situations when you should have guarded your heart and you

didn't. (You don't have to write these at the same time. Reflect and

write what comes to you and revisit as often as you need to.)

- _____

- _____

- _____

- _____

- _____

Are these situations still affecting your life? If so, what are you going to

do to overcome them?

_____

_____

_____

_____

On your own time, write at least two to three goals that YOU are going

to work on to help you guard your heart.

- _____

- _____

- _____

Scriptures to meditate on

☐ "Dear friends, don't be surprised at the fiery trials you are going

through, as if something strange were happening to you.

Instead, be very glad-for these trials make you partners with

Christ in His suffering, so that you will have the wonderful joy

of seeing in His glory when it is revealed to all of the world." (1

Pt 4:12–13 NLT)

☐ ". . . God opposes the proud but gives grace to the humble. So humble yourselves under the mighty power of God, and at the right time He will lift you up in honor. Give all of your worries and cares to God for He cares about you. (1 Pt 5:5–7 NLT)

☐ "Guard your heart above all else, for it determines the course of your life." (Prv 4:23 NLT)

☐ "Don't worry about anything; instead, pray about everything. Tell God what you need and thank Him for all He has done. Then you will experience God's peace, which exceeds anything we can understand. His peace will guard your hearts and minds as you live in Christ Jesus." (Phil 4:6–7 NLT)

☐ "Trust in the Lord with all your heart; do not depend on your own understanding. Seek His will in all you do, and He will show you which path to take." (Prv 3: 5-6 NLT)

☐ "Those who trust in the Lord will find new strength. They will soar high on wings like eagles." (Is 40:31 NLT)

☐ "I know O Lord that your regulations are fair; You disciplined me because I needed it. Now let your unfailing love comfort me, just as you promised me, Your servant." (Ps 119: 75–76 NLT)

☐ "Create in me a clean heart O God, Renew a loyal spirit within me." (Ps 51:10 NLT)

Self-Affirmations:

Girl, Get Up! Look in the mirror or wherever you are and say:

- I am Loved!

- I am forgiven!

- I am strong and mighty!

- I am strong and courageous!

- I am clean and pure!

- I am Protected!

- I have been saved!

- I was born to be more and do more!

- I am God's child!

- I am Important!

Chapter 5: When God Speaks!

When God speaks, you better listen. Do we always listen? Heck no! We get caught up in ourselves and the world, trying to keep up with trends, social media chronicles, or those who said we were not worthy just to prove a point. God speaks to us often and in ways He knows we best receive information. Sometimes He comes through dreams and visions; sometimes He sends people our way, known or unknown; sometimes He talks through our Holy Spirit, which may send a chill down our bodies or a reaction to our hearts or stomachs. Sometimes He may allow something to flash on the radio or television screen, or we may hear a voice. No matter what, He will speak even when we try to ignore the voices and signs or walk around in straight denial or self-pity. Our Father God will discipline us because He loves us. Just as we discipline a loved one because we want the best for him or her, God does the same. Every one of us has a plan and a purpose in this world, so no matter how much we run, we definitely cannot hide from the God who created us.

Does God want us to be happy and live our best life? Of course, He does. He loves when we fellowship and celebrate. It's in His Word. Ecclesiastes 3:9–13 NLT states, *"What do people really get for all their hard work? I have seen the burden God placed on us all. Yet God has made everything beautiful for its own time. He has planted eternity in the human heart, but even so, people cannot see the whole scope of God's work from beginning to end. So, I concluded there is nothing better than to be happy and enjoy ourselves as long as we can. And people should eat and drink and enjoy the fruits of their labor, for these are gifts from God.* When Jesus came down, He celebrated with many, wine and all. In John 2 NLT, Jesus was invited to a wedding, where he went to celebrate and turned water into wine that everyone said was the best wine ever. You see, God wants us to enjoy life. Yes, He wants us to follow Him and let go of some things, and He did not say we have to walk around like zombies in a box. It is hard at times to receive and believe this because of all the distractions and trials that come our way.

The enemy distracted me so much with people blocking my blessings and with financial burdens that I could not focus on what God was calling me to do or trying to bless me with. I don't know if it was depression or not, but the spirit of complacency would creep in and it felt good there. People around me from my church family, some family members and friends, and even strangers spoke about things they saw me doing and told me I was going to be really good at it, but I just could not receive it. One guy I dated told me I had the imposter syndrome and when I looked it up, it was a definition of me. Fear mostly crept in, and I felt I wasn't ready, but year after year, I would hear the same stuff and do nothing about it. Even my older kids said, "Ma, we are getting bigger, and it's time for you to make the money you are supposed to make. You have a doctoral degree, and you are not doing anything with it." When my kids spoke, I knew God was in the midst and that I had to tighten up and get myself together. My church family gave me so many scriptures and prayed over me, but I just couldn't accept that anyone would genuinely want to help me. I would pray, "God, I need help; I need a financial blessing now," but a lot of times I did not get that microwave instantaneous blessing I needed or wanted at that time. I had to recognize that I was not a good steward of my money, and there were some areas in my life that I had to clean up because I made or allowed the mess. The money I would have to pay my tithes or offerings would be spent mainly at Walmart buying food and snacks for my kids, making free dishes for others, which was another source of income, and giving to others what I did not have. I admit I do like helping others and feeding others because I grew up in poverty and I do not like seeing others go without. It brings me joy to put a smile on others' faces and to fill up empty bellies with good food. But when your rent and all the bills you have add up to more than what you are bringing home, sometimes you have to develop self-control and say no or budget. I did neither. I would just spend and pay my bills while my account was in overdraft mode, then cry to God to make sure my overpriced rent went through every month on the overdrawn bank account or to approve a loan so I could make sure my rent got paid without delay. I just kept making a mess. Although my bills were more than what I brought home, I could have put a budget in place. Who is helping the single mom who works and provides for her kids? Not many, and sometimes no one, and so I did have to turn back to God with a humble and sincere heart. Sometimes, I would be too ashamed to ask for help because I felt like an addict month after month in the same situation, circling around the block to the same issues I created or allowed to happen. I had to realize I could not do this alone. I needed help. God has spoken to me so many times about self-control, and I would pretend that I did not hear Him or I would try to block out His voice, so I cannot even blame the devil on this one. The devil might have spearheaded my thought process, but I kept the ball rolling when all along I had the control to stop it.

Consider the book of Jonah. God spoke to Jonah several times to deliver a message to Nineveh, and Jonah felt as if the people didn't deserve a second chance and deserved to be punished. Jonah ran several times until God had to show him that He was still in control by having the whale swallow him. Then in Jonah 2:2 NLT, Jonah said, *"I cried out to the Lord and He answered me. I called to you from the land of the dead and Lord, you heard me!"* Jonah did what he wanted to and ran from God several times, and God forgave him and was patient with him every time. Why? Because God is a loving God, and His Word will not come back void but shall come to pass. God speaks to us in different seasons of our lives. Sometimes we hear something when we are young, but it doesn't make sense until we are grown. Things my mom or grandmother told me when I was younger made no sense, and I made sure to let them know that. I thought I knew it all, Miss Goodie Too Shoes, too smart for her own good, but now as a grown up with kids, I wished I had listened then. Even at times when God speaks to me, I ignore His voice because I want to feel good in the moment I am in, or I want to just lay in my misery. I am learning to listen more and speak less. I am learning to deny myself by fasting on things that I enjoy and surrendering and say "Yes, Lord" instead of trying to get my way all of the time. Let's talk about some women of the Bible. God did not get His

Word out just through the men of the Bible. He either spoke through the women or the women supported the men we know of like Moses, David, and Solomon. Esther is one I love. She was adopted by her uncle, won the King's heart whom she had married and saved her uncle and all of the Jewish people by her faith and boldness. There was Ruth who stood by her mother-in-law's side even after her husband died and was blessed because of her loyalty and faithfulness. There was Rahab, a prostitute in Jericho who risked her life to protect Israelite spies. She not only lied to her king and people, but she also feared the God of the Israelites and was blessed. There are so many more women in the Bible who listened to God and had the courage to do what He said with bravery in a time where men were in full control. Some of these women were deemed as adulterers or sinners, yet God still used them and turned their situations around for the best. If God did it for them, then how much more would He do for you right now?

Just get rid of the noise and listen. God wants to help you and be there for you just like you may want to provide the best and be there for your kids, family, or friends. What is it that you are running from or trying to ignore? Do you have the gift to prophesy or interpret visions? Are you an author or poet with gifts to share with the world? Are you supposed to go to college, a vocational school, or training to improve the craft and gifts God gave to you but are running away because you have too many distractions? Are you being told to leave a relationship or pursue a new relationship but won't because of fear? Some of us are saying we do not have enough money to just survive, yet we are sitting on gifts God put inside of us to use that would triple our income. We get complacent in certain jobs, tasks, or relationships and feel stuck, as if millions of people are holding us back. There will be distractions, demonic squatters, and trials that will be thrown into our paths and cause us to pause at times, but don't get stuck there. Whenever there is a test or assignment for us, God will speak. He will retest us every time we fail until we pass that test. When we do pass the test, we understand the meaning and purpose of it. It may not feel good going through the process, but once we make it, we are not only relieved but also blessed with wisdom and understanding. Whatever it is you are running from, God did not create us to suffer and not enjoy the world He made. Just like for your kids, loved ones, and significant other, we want the best for them and will provide for and love them unconditionally even when they do us wrong. Don't you know God will do even more than that! Just trust His process and listen to His voice, so **Girl, Get Up and walk in**

your blessings!

Prayer to help you along the way:

Dear Heavenly Father, I need to hear Your voice and feel Your presence right now. Let Your voice speak to me and tell me what I ought to do or say. I surrender to You now my Lord because I am tired of running and of the constant warfare that seems to never fade away. Give me the resources, people, and the strength to carry out this vision you have laid on my heart. Remove those people or things that will set me back and steer me from what I am supposed to do. Lord, may you receive the glory as I do Your will. Do not forsake your daughter dear Lord. Listen to my cry and answer me, in Jesus' name, Amen!

Self-Reflection:

So, what is God speaking to you about? Write down your story as if you were telling it to a very good friend or family member. When you talk to God, tell Him exactly how you feel. Let the words flow.

_____

_____

_____

_____

_____

_____

_____

_____

_____

_____

_____

_____

_____

_____

_____

_____

_____

_____

_____

_____

_____

_____

_____

List some things God has told you. (You don't have to write these at the same time. Reflect and write what comes to you and revisit as often as you need to.)

- _____

- _____

- _____

- _____

- _____

Do you have a Jonah spirit and run? Has fear crept in? Did God tell you to do something? Did He tell you to leave someone or something? If so, what are you going to do about it?

On your own time, write at least two to three goals that YOU are going to work on what God has spoken to you about.

- _____

- _____

- _____

Scriptures to meditate on:

☐ "My children, listen when your Father corrects you. Pay attention and learn good judgment, for I am giving you good guidance." (Prv 4: 1–2 NLT)

☐ "My sheep hear My voice; I know them and they follow Me." (John 10:27 NLT)

☐ "Anyone who belongs to God listens gladly to the words of God." (John 8:47 NLT)

☐ "The Spirit alone gives eternal life. Human effort accomplishes nothing. And the very words I have spoken to you are spirit and life." (John 6:63 NLT)

☐   "When the Spirit of truth comes, He will guide you into all truth. He will not speak on His own but will tell you what He has heard. He will tell you about the future." (John 16:13 NLT)

☐   "All Scripture is inspired by God and is useful to teach us what is true and to make us realize what is wrong in our lives. It corrects us when we are wrong and teaches us to do what is right. God uses us to prepare and equip His people to do every good work." (2 Tm 3:16–17 NLT)

☐   "I am the Lord. Is anything too hard for Me?" (Jer 32:27 NLT)

☐   "Ask me and I will tell remarkable secrets you do not know about things to come." (Jer 33:3 NLT)

☐   "This is the way you should go." (Is 30:21 NLT)

☐   "He alone is my refuge, my place of safety. (Ps 91:22 NLT)

☐   "Sing praises to God our strength." (Ps 81:1 NLT)

☐   "My victory and honor come from God alone." (Ps 62:7 NLT)

Self-Affirmations:

Girl, Get Up! Look in the mirror or wherever you are and say:

*   I am chosen!

*   I am treasured!

*   I am God's masterpiece!

*   I am beautiful and made wonderfully!

*   I am God's child!

*   I am not forgotten!

*   He loves me-flaws and all-just the way I am!

*   I am blessed!

*   I will receive what's mine in God's timing!

*   God gave me strength to do all things!

*   I will win!

*   I am a winner!

Chapter 6: Personal Vision and Growth

When one of my friends from church told me about a dream she had where she saw me holding on tightly to God, I went back to the story of Esau and Jacob where Jacob was holding the heel of his twin Esau and when he told God he was not letting go until God blessed him. I thought that was a good thing, but living day to day, I still felt stuck and unblessed. Yes, God wants us to draw near to Him, but He also wants us to let Him go as we would want our children to let go and move on with their lives. Being stuck and holding on to God like a baby just starting school can be tough, but once we believe He is there and we let go, we grow and receive so much more.

So, what is it that you want or want to do? What is holding you back from achieving your vision? Is your vision to write, sing, dance, or travel? Do you want to finish school or get a degree despite feeling you are too old to do so? Do you want to learn a trade, model, or design your own clothing? Whatever it is you envision at whatever age, pray about it and ask God to bless you with it. That vision didn't just come out of nowhere because it is something that you must do or will do now or in the future. There are things that God has given us because He heard our prayers or He already has a plan that we must carry out. We sit and complain, become complacent or discouraged and we keep praying and crying out to God because we want a magical experience instantly. In Exodus 14:15 (NLT), God said to Moses, *"Why are you crying out to me? Tell the people to get moving!"* God gave us the power to do what we need to or are supposed to do. Just as our own kids or family members may have some of our features, characteristics, and gifts, the same is that for us because God is our Father and we have the power to move things because it is in our blood. Don't get discouraged when the thing we want to happen is not microwavable and instant. The seed was planted in your heart and is now ready to sprout.

The gifts, talents, and visions that come to you are for you. Sometimes we share our visions and gifts with others. This can be good and bad. The good outcome from sharing your vision is that others will inspire and encourage you along the way, cheering you on and supporting you throughout the process. It's a beautiful thing when people are there to support you and cheer you on and are not looking for anything but for you to win. Ecclesiastes 4: 9–10 12 NLT, says, *"Two people are better off than one, for they can help each other succeed. If one person falls, the other can reach out and help. But someone who falls alone is in real trouble. A person standing alone can be attacked and defeated, but two can stand back-to-back and conquer. Three are even better, for a triple-braided cord is not easily broken."* When God sets the tone and we allow Him to lead, then things will fall into place. Everyone needs or wants support from others, no matter how independent they think they are or perceive themselves to be. The support can come in the form of sharing information on social media, passing out fliers, designing crafts to distribute, helping out with a fundraiser, or even just being in the audience or showing up at your important event. No matter how strong I thought my guard was and how tough I acted, when I saw those who rooted for me or heard their voices, my heart was receptive to the love, and all I could do was smile. I thank God for the family and friends that will show up and show out for me because the love is genuine and they want me to win like I want others to win.

The bad outcome of sharing your personal vision and growth with others is that jealousy, envy, and curses may come along. Some people will even steal your vision or try to jump on the bandwagon just to say they did it first (when they really just want to beat you at what you put out). Now there will be times when you share your personal vision with others and realize you share the same vision. That's okay because great minds do think a lot. Sometimes they may fulfill their vision before you, but that's okay too because that just means that your season has not come yet. There is no need to be jealous or envious because your gifts are your gifts, and what God has for you is for you! The happiness others have for you may turn into hatred, jealousy, or envy. These people will speak curses over your vision and life. Every time they see you, they get mad and may even start gossiping or spreading rumors about you. When you start sharing with people you think may be happy for you and will celebrate with you, pay attention to your Holy Spirit. If you get that tingling feeling, butterflies in your stomach, a chill, or just feel like a bad cloud just came over you, then stop talking immediately. Those are not the people you want to share your vision with. The best thing to do is pray for what you want with a spirit of expectancy. I remember when God started moving me so He could elevate me to another level with a more positive mindset. Some people wanted me to stay where I was, but it was time to grow and move on. I got tired of doing the same thing every day, and I found myself gossiping more and becoming more complacent even though I knew I was created to do and be more. I had some depression in the midst, and I was so disgusted with myself. I told God to either move me from my workplace or to another position; to mend relationships with family members and distant friends or remove them from my life, and He did that. With the move came the comments from a few: "Oh, you are changing; you're a fake Christian or hypocrite; you're no saint; you deserved the abuse you received", and the list goes on. I often heard the "you're changing" comment when a lot of people moved from different positions, got into a Greek organization, or just advanced to another level. Sometimes those new levels of change or elevation did make them seem different, in both a positive and negative way, depending on their actions in different seasons of their lives. At first, I took those comments to mean something negative, but as I reflected, I noticed I did change. I changed because I got tired of doing the same things over and over. I got tired of hearing myself complain, my spirit started feeling yucky, and it was reflective of me from the inside out. It was time for me to grow and elevate, and my church family poured that encouragement into me often. Change is good because as I get older, I am supposed to grow wiser and be able to pour into others. God will let you know who to share your vision with, or He may tell you to be quiet as you go through the process of fulfilling the vision He laid on your heart.

There were a lot of times when I would try to do things my way and wanted to do everything at once so I could be done with the process in one step, but God would tell me no and would take His time molding me step by step. God's process of course is better because it allowed me to see each area in my life that I needed to work on and why, which would create in me a humble spirit and grateful heart. If you face trials during your vision process, then it is something God wants to grow you through, so don't get discouraged, or better yet, "stay there". Sometimes we get overexcited to prove ourselves to others, and that is the wrong attitude. Sometimes we get overexcited to be starting our own business or a new project, and when the outcome does not come out as expected, we get discouraged, depressed, angry, and we quit. All billionaires and millionaires were not handed down success. Many of them started from the bottom by themselves or with a small support team, and they did not quit. Blow after blow, they did not give up and now have the best or are labeled as the best. They started with a vision and believed with faith that they were going to be successful, and their vision came true. Your vision is your vision, so don't sleep on it too long. You might see others around you flourish in their seasons with your ideas or similar ideas, but do not get discouraged. Your season is your season, so don't ignore it because you do not know when the next one will come around.

A prayer to help you along the way:

Dear Heavenly Father, I thank You for creating me with gifts and talents that will glorify You. Thank You for deeming me as Yours and allowing me to make choices that may hurt, but in the long run, will be beneficial to me and others. Father, You said I am the apple of your eye and that You will fulfill my plans and visions and I want to believe that wholeheartedly so please Lord help me in the areas of my unbelief and lack of faith so that I can receive all of the blessings You have in store for me. I wait patiently Lord to hear from You so I will know how to proceed with the blessings You have for me. May my heart stay humble and may You receive all of the Glory. I pray this and receive it in Jesus's name, Amen!

Self-Reflection:

So, what are your visions? Write them down. When you talk to God, tell

Him exactly how you want Him to help you with your gifts and talents.

_____

_____

_____

_____

_____

_____

_____

_____

_____

_____

_____

_____

_____

_____

_____

_____

_____

_____

_____

_____

_____

_____

_____

_____

_____

List five personal visions you have or create a vision board and watch

your visions come to life. (You don't have to write these at the same

time. Reflect and write what comes to you and revisit as often as you

need to.)

- _____

- _____

- _____

- _____

- _____

On your own time, write at least two to three goals that YOU are going

to do to fulfill your personal visions.

- _____

- _____

- _____

Scriptures to meditate on:

☐ "I know the plans I have for you, says the Lord…Plans for good and not for disaster, to give you a future and a hope." (Jer 29:11 NLT)

☐ "At just the right time we will reap a harvest of blessing if we don't give up." (Gal 6:9 NLT)

☐ "Oh, that you would bless me and expand my territory! Please be with me in all that I do and keep me from all trouble and pain! (1 Chr 4: 10 NLT)

☐ I can do all things through Christ who strengthens me." (Phil 4:13 NLT)

☐ "When your faith remains strong through many trials, it will bring you much praise and glory and honor on the day when Jesus Christ is revealed." (1 Pt 1:7 NLT)

☐ "Always pray and never give up." (Luke 18:1 NLT)

☐ "God has not given us a spirit of fear and timidity, but of power, love, and self-discipline." (2 Tm 1:7 NLT)

☐ "Work willingly at whatever you do, as though you were working for the Lord rather than for people." (Col 3:23 NLT)

☐ "It is good for people to eat, drink, and enjoy their work under the sun during the short life God has given them, and to accept their lot in life. And it is a good thing to receive wealth from God and the good health to enjoy it. To enjoy your work and accept your lot in life-this is indeed a gift from God. God keeps such people so busy enjoying life that they take no time to brood over the past." (Eccl 5:18–20 NLT)

☐ "Those who plant in tears will harvest with shouts of joy." (Ps 126:5 NLT)

☐   "Commit your actions to the Lord and your plans will succeed."

(Prv 16:3 NLT)

Self-Affirmations:

Girl, Get Up! Look in the mirror or wherever you are and say:

- God created me to do more.

- I will use the gifts God blessed me with.

- I excel in all things that's for me.

- What God has for me is for me.

- I am fruitful, powerful, strong, and healthy.

- I have favor from my Heavenly Father.

- I am not a procrastinator.

- I am celebrated and loved.

- God chose me to do His works.

Chapter 7: Steps to Better You

Have Faith.

Have faith in God and what He will do in your life. He wants to bless you abundantly and restore the blessings you have lost. Believe that what He said in His Word will come to fruition. Believe also in yourself. So many times, we beat ourselves up, thinking the worst of ourselves. **YOU MATTER!** You were not created to be nothing or no one, but to matter and be all that you can be. You were made to do more and to show the world that God created someone beautiful and wonderful!

Reflect.

Reflection can be hard at times, especially when you only see things from your perspective. There will be times when others may have an opinion about you because you are not indulging in their selfish ways, but there will be times when more than one person will say the same thing about you. Listen to what they say and reflect. There are times when you may seem unapproachable, and then you are in your feelings because you feel like no one has said anything to you. They wanted to, but based on your demeanor and past comments, they may just stand back and allow you to do you. Sometimes, they may vent to some of your close family members or friends, and this may seem like gossiping. Are they ganging up on you to be mean and envious, or are they helping or wanting to help you identify something about yourself you may be in denial about? Don't take everything to heart, especially when others want to see you grow and excel in all that you do. Reflect, and find an accountable friend or family member who is going to keep it real with you and not offend or demean you in any way. With love, you will receive some good information about you that will help you become a better you.

Develop Self-Control/Discipline.

"But God's discipline is always good for us, so that we might share in His holiness. No discipline is enjoyable while it is happening-it's painful! But afterward, there will be a peaceful harvest of right living for those who are trained in this way." (Heb 12:10-11 NLT) Having self-control is one of the hardest things to accomplish. Self-control can have different meanings and purposes for the person who needs to develop it. I have had so many areas in my life where I have had to develop self-control, even when it was eating me alive to control myself.

Many times, I would go back and forth with those I felt did me wrong or with whom I had to prove they were wrong, and I was right. I would stand my ground and defend myself against those who took advantage of me or jabbed me in a corner long enough that I felt I had no choice but to explode, or so I felt. I have accomplished developing self-control with my body, but that mind and tongue of my mind, ohhhhh, is taking some work. Every day is a battlefield, and some days are worse than others, especially when you do not equip yourself with the tools and strategies to fight the many demonic spirits walking all around you, ready to capture you and take control. There were times when I would leave a dispute or text and then drive or go home and reflect on more stuff I should have said. The few times that I did that, I realized I accomplished nothing but more distance from the other party, hatred towards the person, and anger that started affecting my health. There were times that I chewed others up with my words and then felt condemned because there were not enough apologies to make the person feel better or trust me not to hurt him or her again. I may have won the argument or dispute, but I lost myself and what I stood for. How can I call myself a disciple of Christ when I am ready to go to war with my words or even my silence? They say hurt people hurt, and my actions would show that.

I would walk right past someone as if I didn't know him or her, puffing up my chest as if I had done something great. Maybe in the flesh I did, but I would often feel my Spirit letting me know I was wrong even though I was right.

Having the last word or even apologizing when you and God know that you were right is not always a good feeling. I had to learn to stop and shut up. "Girl!" is what I would often say to myself when I had enough of hearing me get nowhere with others who were not on the same path as me. Why waste my time with people who have nothing to lose or have no care about jail or death? Everyone is fighting against one or more evil spirits, and so I had to realize I wasn't the only one, so instead of always trying to win, I developed empathy for others, even when they did not deserve it. Not only did I have to develop self-control with my words and thought patterns but also with my spending, my enjoyment of sex, and the time I gave to playing strategic games on my phone. I would judge others for being on social media from sunrise to sunset, but I was no better. As soon as I would get frustrated, I would pull out that phone and spend hours playing games, even spending money to purchase power-ups, acting like a feen. I had to learn to deny myself of things my flesh wanted, which wasn't easy, but it helped me seek more of God and less of myself.

When you reflect, observe your situation and what you need to do to develop self-control. It could be controlling your tongue or thought pattern. Maybe it is weening yourself off social media or phone/video games or spending less money on material things and eating out. Could it be that you need to stand up and say no to family members or friends who want you to go somewhere or do something with or for them, depriving yourself of sleep, energy, and funds? Go into fasting and sacrifice something to show God that you are willing to do His will and develop a closer relationship with Him. Day by day, work on fading out something or limiting your time and energy on something or someone that is distracting you from your vision or goal. Make developing self-control a good habit so you can focus more on God and on people or things that matter in the long run.

Listen. *"...Look after each other so that none of you fails to receive the grace of God. Watch out that no poisonous root of bitterness grows up to trouble you, corrupting many."* (Heb 12:15 NLT) There are times when we want to be heard so bad that we do not listen. I tell my children and students all the time, *"If you are not listening, then you are not learning."* Jesus says in one of his parables in Mark 4: 24-25 NLT,

"...Pay close attention to what you hear. The closer you listen, the more understanding you will be given-and you will receive even more. To those who listen to My teaching, more understanding will be given. But for those who are not listening, even what little understanding they have will be taken away from them." We want to be the only voice in the room, standing our ground, fighting for someone to apologize to us, seeking to cause pain that was given to us, all the while not listening or being fair. Even if you are right about the situation, there is a lot to learn when we listen. Listen and reflect on what the person said, and maybe at some point in your life, you will be able to forgive and move past the situation. Every situation does not require a response or reaction. Instead of being quick to offer advice or speak from your perspective with words of encouragement, just take the time to listen. That person may be at a point in their lives where no words can soothe their spirit. They may need to vent and have you just listen. Everyone needs a listening ear. Listen when God is speaking to you. Sometimes we think we are hearing voices, but God does speak to us. Just hush the noise and listen. What is it He is telling you to do or change? James 1:19 NLT says, *"Understand this, my dear brothers and sisters: You must all be quick to listen, slow to speak, and slow to get angry."* You will learn so much about yourself

and others when you take the time to sit back and listen, which will help you become less judgmental and have more empathy.

Expect to be blessed.

My elder at church would always say, "Come with a spirit of expectancy." Believe that you are blessed and expect those blessings to come through. We are so used to focusing on the negative, the what-nots, that we forget to speak life into our situations and expect to receive positive results because we can have more if we expect to be given more. If you keep having thoughts pop up in your head to write that book, trademark your hair or T-shirt brand, start your own business, or change careers, then create a plan, a vision board, or anything that allows you to visually see your vision manifest. God wants to bless us abundantly, but we have to listen, gain wisdom and understanding, and develop self-control. We get ourselves in situations because we want to do it our way and then we get mad and blame God when He does not bless us accordingly. With a humble heart, pray over your vision and expect it to flourish. Rebuke fear and those who speak against you. Stay humble and expect to be blessed.

Prayer to help you along the way:

Father God, it is your daughter again. I come to you first thanking You for all You have done, are doing, and will continue to do for me. You said in Your Word that I am Yours and that You do want me to be happy and live a purpose driven life and that you will give me the desires of my heart. Lord, I ask in Jesus' name that You give me more of You and less of me so that I am able to see the plans and fulfill the visions that You lay on my heart. Father, You believe in me to glorify You in my walk and through the gifts and talents You have given me. Walk with me Lord as I fulfill the plans You have for me because Your Word will not come back void. I thank You for the plans you have for me, the paths I will walk to fulfill these plans and the wisdom to discern with a humble spirit, in Jesus' name, Amen!

Self-Reflection:

So, what steps are you going to implement to better yourself?

_____

_____

_____

_____

_____

_____

_____

_____

_____

_____

_____

_____

_____

_____

_____

_____

_____

_____

_____

_____

_____

_____

_____

_____

_____

List five steps you would like to focus on to better yourself. (You don't have to write these at the same time. Reflect and write what comes to you and revisit as often as you need to.)

- _____

- _____

- _____

- _____

- _____

On your own time, write at least two to three goals that YOU are going to work on to help guide you to bettering yourself.

- _____

- _____

Scriptures to meditate on:

☐ "Plant the good seeds of righteousness and you will harvest a crop of love." (Hos 10:12 NLT)

☐ "Create in me a clean heart O God. Renew a loyal spirit within me." (Ps 51:10 NLT)

☐ "Those who plant in tears will harvest with shouts of joy." (Ps 126:5 NLT)

☐ "Oh that you would bless me and expand my territory! Please be with me in all that I do and keep me from all trouble and pain! (1 Chr 4: 10 NLT)

☐ I can do all things through Christ who strengthens me." (Phil 4:13 NLT)

- "Taste and see that the Lord is good. Oh, the joys of those who take refuge in Him." (Ps 34:8 NLT)

- "The earnest prayer of a righteous person has great power." (Jas 5:16 NLT)

- "Do to others as you would like them to do to you." (Luke 6:31 NLT)

- "Keep on asking and you will receive what you ask for. Keep on seeking and you will find. Keep on knocking and the door will be opened to you." (Mt 7:7 NLT)

- "Seek the kingdom of God above all else, and live righteously, and He will give you everything you need." (Mt 6:33 NLT)

- "Fear of the Lord is the foundation of wisdom. Knowledge of the Holy One results in good judgment." (Prv 9:10 NLT)

☐ "Taste and see that the Lord is good. Oh, the joys of those who take refuge." (Ps 34:8 NLT)

☐ "O Lord, oppose those who oppose me. Fight against those who fight against me." (Ps 35:1 NLT)

☐ "Take control of what I say O Lord and guard my lips. Don't let me drift toward evil or take part in acts of wickedness. Don't let me share in the delicacies of those who do wrong." (Ps 141: 3–4 NLT)

☐ "Give thanks to the Lord for He is good! His faithful love endures forever." (Ps 118: 1 NLT)

☐ "You made me; you create me. Now give me the sense to follow your commands." (Ps 119: 73 NLT)

☐ "We are pressed on every side by troubles, but we are not crushed. We are perplexed but not driven to despair. We are hunted down, but never abandoned by God. We get knocked down, but we are not destroyed. Through suffering, our bodies continue to share in the death of Jesus so that the life of Jesus may be seen in our bodies." (II Cor 4: 8–10 NLT)

☐ "As long as he sought the Lord, God made him to prosper." (II Chr 26:5 NLT)

☐ "The Lord is able to give you much more than this!" (II Chr 25:9 NLT)

☐ "O our God, we do not know what to do, but we are looking to You for help." (II Chr 20:12 NLT)

☐ "We have the Lord our God to help us and to fight our battles for us." (II Chr 32:8 NLT)

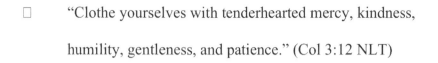

☐ "Clothe yourselves with tenderhearted mercy, kindness, humility, gentleness, and patience." (Col 3:12 NLT)

Self-Affirmations:

Girl, Get Up! Look in the mirror or wherever you are and say:

- I am Amazing!

- I am God's Masterpiece!

- I Matter!

- I know I will be blessed!

- I know I am blessed!

- I know I am a blessing!

- I am Unique!

- There is only one me!

- I am a Proverbs 31 Woman!

Songs to minister to or to get you through:

- "The Lord's Song" by Maranda Curtis

- "Is My Living in Vain" by The Clark Sisters

- "Hang On in There" by Kierra Sheard

- "Life & Favor: You Don't Know My Story" by John P. Kee and New Life

- "Help" by Erica Campbell, featuring Lacrae

- "The Question" by Erica Campbell

- "Lead Me to the Rock-Reprise" by Stephen Hurd

- "8:28" by Lecrae

- "He Will Supply" by Kirk Franklin

- "Everyone Hurts" by Kirk Franklin

- "You Remain" (featuring Chandler Moore) by Todd Galberth

- "Praying for You" by Lacrae

- "You're the Lifter-Live Ricky Dillard

- "I Won't Complain" by Reverend Paul Jones

- "The Blessing" (feat. Kari Jobe & Cody Carnes) by Elevation Worship

- "Healer" by William Murphy

- ☐ "Encouragement Medley-My Worship Is For Real" by VaShawn Mitchell

- ☐ "Standing In The Need" by New Life Community Choir

- ☐ "Hope" by Jonathan Traylor

- ☐ "I Believe" by Shawn McLemore

- ☐ "Free (Live)" (feat. BRL) by Kierra Sheard

- ☐ "More Than I Can Bear" by God's Property from Kirk Franklin's Nu Nation

- ☐ "All I Need" by Brian Courtney Wilson

- ☐ "Brokenhearted" by Kirk Franklin

- ☐ "Like Never Before (Live)" by Shekinah Glory Ministry

- ☐ "All in Your Hands" by Marvin Sapp

Songs to jam to while you're cleaning or driving (Keep your mind focused on HIM):

- ☐ "A Little More Jesus" by Erica Campbell

- ☐ "Go Get It" by Mary Mary

- ☐ "Here Right Now" by Tasha Page-Lockhart

- ☐ "I Made It" (ft. Tye Tribbett) by Fantasia

- ☐ "Unstoppable" by Koryn Hawthorne ft. Lacrae

- ☐ "Speak to Me (Queen Mix)" by Koryn Hawthorne & Queen Naija
- ☐ 2nd Win by Kierra Sheard
- ☐ "Best Work" by Tasha Page-Lockhart
- ☐ "Restore Me Again" by Deitrick Haddon
- ☐ "God's Got a Blessing with My Name on It" by Norman Hutchins
- ☐ "What Matters" by Kierra Sheard ft. Mali Music
- ☐ "Black Sheep Freestyle by Pastor Mike Jr.
- ☐ "I Will Follow" by Tasha Cobbs Leonard
- ☐ "Set Me Free" (featuring YK Osiris) by Lacrae
- ☐ "They Ain't Know" by Lacrae
- ☐ "Big (Extended Version)" by Pastor Mike Jr
- ☐ "So Good" by Pastor Mike Jr.
- ☐ "I Got It" by Pastor Mike Jr.
- ☐ "Talkin Bout Love" (feat Lizzie Morgan) by Maverick City Music & Kirk Franklin
- ☐ "Restored" (feat. 1K Phew, Wande & Hulvey) by Lacrae
- ☐ "Feenin" (feat. Skoolie Escobar) by Pastor Mike Jr.
- ☐ "Miracles" (feat. Pastor Mike Jr.) by Kierra Sheard

- "Sunday Morning" (feat. Kirk Franklin) by Lecrae

- "Give Me" (feat. Mali Music) by Kirk Franklin

God has the final say songs:

- "Something Has to Break" by Kierra Sheard and Tasha Cobbs-Leonard

- "It's Not Over" by Karen Clark-Sheard

- "Good & Bad" by J Moss

- Second Chance by Hezekiah Walker

- "Can't Give Up" by Mary Mary

- "War Cry" by Queen Naija

- "Something Out of Nothing" by Jessica Reedy

- "I Am God" by Donald Lawrence and the Tri-City Singers

- "Still Here" by 21:03

- "Justified" by Smokie Norful

- "The Blood Will Never Lose Its Power" by Smokie Norful

- "God, Turn it Around" by Jon Reddick

- "I'm Still Here" by The Williams Brothers

- "I'll Find You" feat. Tori Kelly by Lacrae

- "Never Lost a Battle" by CeCe Winans

- ☐ "The Battle is Not Yours" by Yolanda Adams

- ☐ "Grace" (feat. Leandria Johnson) by Charles Jenkins & Fellowship Chicago

- ☐ "He Won't Fail" by Marvin Sapp

Recognizing & Loving YOU:

- ☐ "You Say" by Lauren Daigle

- ☐ "He Knows My Name" by Tasha Cobb-Leonard

- ☐ "My Flaws" by Kierra Sheard

- ☐ "Different" by Tasha Page-Lockhart

- ☐ "Cranes in the Sky" by Solange

- ☐ "Blessed & Highly Favored" by The Clark Sisters

- ☐ "Good Morning Gorgeous" by Mary J. Blige

- ☐ "Love Me Naked" by Ella Mai

- ☐ "Imagine Me" by Alexis Spight

- ☐ "I Try" by DOE

- ☐ "Cry" by Koryn Hawthorne

- ☐ "It Keeps Happening (Live)" by Kierra Sheard

- ☐ "Things You Do" by Kierra Sheard

- ☐ "Mo' Better" by Kierra Sheard"

- ☐ Beautiful" by Kierra Sheard

- ☐ "Peace" (feat. Jonathan McReynolds) by Koryn Hawthorne

- ☐ "LOL, SMH" by Pastor Mike Jr.

- ☐ "I'm Changing" by William Murphy

- ☐ 'Free Indeed" by William Murphy

Songs of surrendering:

- ☐ "Change Me" by Tamela Mann

- ☐ "A Touch From You" by Tamela Mann

- ☐ "I Desire More" by Crystal Aikin

- ☐ "Deliver Me" by Donald Lawrence

- ☐ "Yes" by Shekinah Glory

- ☐ "Fill Me Up" by Tasha Cobb-Leonard

- ☐ "Craving" by Tye Tribbett

- ☐ "It's Time" (feat. Tasha Page-Lockhart) by Kirk Franklin

- ☐ "Make Me Over" by Tonex

- ☐ "Wait" by Nia Allen

- ☐ "He Wants It All" by Doe

- ☐ "When I Pray" by DOE

- ☐ "I Surrender (Reprise)" [Live] by Psalmist Raine

- ☐ "All Yours" (featuring Anthony Brown) by Kierra Sheard

- ☐ "Cry For You" (featuring Taylor Hill) by Lacrae

- ☐ "Yes Reprise" by Shekinah Glory

- ☐ "I Trust You Testimony" by James Fortune & FIYA

- ☐ "Give Me You (live)" by Shana Wilson

- ☐ "First Love" by Kirk Franklin

- ☐ "Intercession" by Kirk Franklin

- ☐ "I Need You" by The Walls Group

- ☐ "Forever at Your Feet" (feat. William Murphy) by Tasha Cobb-Leonard

- ☐ "Make Room" by Jonathan McReynolds

- ☐ "Oceans (Where Feet May Fail)" by Hillsong UNITED

- ☐ "Order My Steps" by GMWA Women of Worship

- ☐ "I Will Wait by Bri (Briana Babineaux)

- ☐ "Try Love" by Kirk Franklin

- ☐ "Father Knows Best" by Kirk Franklin

- ☐ "It's Working" by Williams Murphy

- ☐ "Revelation 4" (Radion Edit) (Live) by Todd Dulaney

- ☐ "Comfort Zone" by Marvin Sapp

- ☐ "Dear God (Live)" by Smokie Norful

- ☐ "Made a Way" by Travis Greene

Songs of praise and rejoicing:

- ☐ We Must Praise" by James Moss

- ☐ "Lord You've Been So Good" by Amber Bullock

- ☐ "God Has Smiled on Me" by Mary Mary

- ☐ Awe of You (Reprise) by J.J. Hairston & Youthful Praise

- ☐ "Jesus, Jesus, Jesus" by Timothy Wright

- ☐ "The Name" (featuring Brandon Lake & Maryanne) by Maverick City Music & Kirk Franklin

- ☐ "Victory Belongs to Jesus (Reprise) by Todd Dulaney

- ☐ "Matters (instead of complaining, praise Him)" by Brent Jones (CCM)

- ☐ Grateful (remix) by Hezekiah Walker & The Love Fellowship Crusade

- ☐ "Praise Break" by William Murphy

- ☐ "More (Reprise)" [feat. Tashawna Johnson] by Lawrence Flowers & Intercession

- ☐ "It Could Be Worse" by James Fortune

- ☐ "My Hands Are Lifted Up" by Bri (Briana Babineaux)

- "Brighter" by DOE

- "Something God" by William Murphy

- "Amazing" by Pastor Mike Jr.

- "Your Great Name" Todd Dulaney

- "I Need More" by Shekinah Glory Ministry

- "Now Behold the Lamb" by Kirk Franklin

- "Forever/Beautiful Grace" by Kirk Franklin

- "Let Your Power Fall" (feat Zacardi Cortez) by James Fortune

- "Your Power" by Lacrae & Tasha Cobb- Leonard

- "Jireh" by Elevation Worship & Maverick City

- "Yes, Lord, Yes" by Shirley Ceasar

- "Who Would Have Thought" by Donnie McClurkin

- "Here" by Tasha Cobb-Leonard

- "You Deserve It" (feat. Bishop Cortez Vaughn) by J.J. Hairston & Youthful Praise

Get Up Scriptures! God is calling you higher!

"Get up and prepare for action…" (Jer 1:17 NLT)

"But forget all that- it is nothing compared to what I am going to do. For I am about to do something new…" (Isa 43: 18-19 NLT)

But those who trust in the Lord will find new strength. They will soar high on wings like eagles. They will run and not grow weary. They will walk and not faint. (Isa 40:31 NLT)

The righteous keep moving forward, and those with clean hands become stronger and stronger. (Job 17: 9 NLT)

The Lord says, "I will guide you along the best pathway for your life. I will advise you and watch over you." (Ps 32:8 NLT)

So be strong and courageous all who put your hope in the Lord! (Ps 31:24 NLT)

"Stand up in the presence of the elderly and show respect for the aged. Fear your God. I am the Lord your God." (Lev 19: 32 NLT)

Then the Lord said to Moses, "Why are you crying out to me? Tell the people to get moving!" (Ex 14:15 NLT)

"When we were at Mount Sinai, the Lord our God said to us, "You have stayed at this mountain long enough. It is time to break camp and move on…" (Deut 1:6-7 NLT)

Look straight ahead, and fix your eyes on what lies before you. (Prov 4:25 NLT

Commit your actions to the Lord, and your plans will succeed. (Prov 16:3 NLT

"I know the plans I have for you," says the Lord…"Plans for good and not for disaster, to give you a future and a hope." (Jer 29:11 NLT)

Jesus told him, "Get up, take up your bed, and walk!" (John 5:8 ESV)

But my life is worth nothing to me unless I use it for finishing the work assigned me by the Lord Jesus-the work of telling others the Good News about the wonderful grace of God. (Acts 20: 24 NLT)

And we know that God causes everything to work together for the good of those who love God and are called according to His purpose for them. (Rom 8:28 NLT)

Don't copy the behavior and customs of this world, but let God transform you into a new person by changing the way you think. Then you will learn to know God's will for you, which is good and pleasing and perfect. (Rom 12:2 NLT)

…But I press on to possess that perfection for which Jesus Christ first possessed me…I have not achieved it, but I focus on this one thing: Forgetting the past and looking forward to what lies ahead, I press on to reach the end of the race and receive the Heavenly prize for which God, through Christ Jesus, is calling us. (Phil 3:12-14 NLT)

…Fix your thoughts on what is true and honorable, and right, and pure, and lovely, and admirable. Think about things that are excellent and worthy of praise. Keep putting into practice all you learned and received from me-everything you heard from me and saw me doing. Then the God of peace will be with you. (Phil 4: 8-9 NLT)

"Get up, for it is your duty to tell us how to proceed in setting things straight. We are behind you, so be strong and take action." (Ezra 10:4 NLT)

Conclusion

I really hope this book ministers to your spirit. It's not easy living in this world at times, especially when you have not healed from childhood traumas and the present traumas that you are presented with. Some things like depression, distractions, disappointments, and heartaches will come and go, but so will peace, joy, happiness, wisdom, and love. Some situations will have you circling the block because it's something God wants to grow you through, and some situations, with wisdom and understanding, will allow you to stand your ground before they come your way. There will be times you will have faith in some areas of your life, and sometimes you will have little to no faith because fear has taken over. You knew the answer, but because you were scared, you just allowed yourself to lose. Don't be discouraged. You are human, and life will happen with the good and the bad. Let us use this book to empower one another. So, girl, get up! You got this!

About the author

Melanie is a single mother of six children, four boys and twin girls, each with their very own personality and unique style. She is a special education teacher and enjoys working with children. She enjoys writing, cooking, and fellowshipping with family and friends. This is her first published book. There are more to come!

Want me to come speak at your event or to setup as a vendor, then email me at blessed1enterprise@gmail.com

About the Illustrator:

Illustrator: Gregory Green

Gregory is the founder of Blessed Graphix Inc., where for over 14 years as a business, he's created artwork and digital designs for clients ranging from small business owners to Florida State Representatives.

He's self-taught and has illustrated multiple book covers as well as children's book series such as "ReadMan" and "I am GOD's work of art".   www. BlessedGraphix .net / Instagram - @BlessedGraphix

Made in the USA
Columbia, SC
24 March 2024

33544709R00070